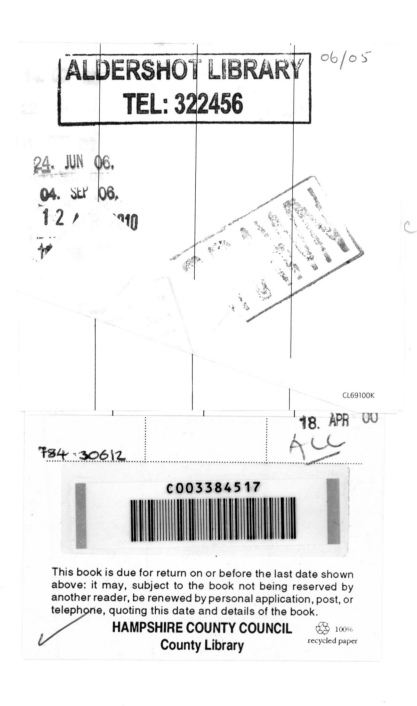

All Woman Cabaret

Production:Sadie Cook
Published 1996

© International Music Publications Limited
Southend Road, Woodford Green, Essex IG8 8HN, England

All Woman Cabaret

ALL THE WAY

Words and Music by SAMMY CAHN
and JAMES VAN HEUSEN

© 1957 Maraville Music Corp, USA
The International Music Network Ltd, Buckhurst Hill, Essex IG9 5NS

4

ALMOST LIKE BEING IN LOVE

Words by ALAN JAY LERNER
Music by FREDERICK LOEWE

ANOTHER OPENIN', ANOTHER SHOW

Words and Music by
COLE PORTER

ANYTHING GOES

Words and Music by
COLE PORTER

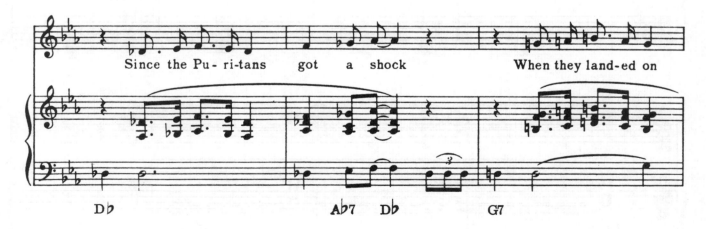

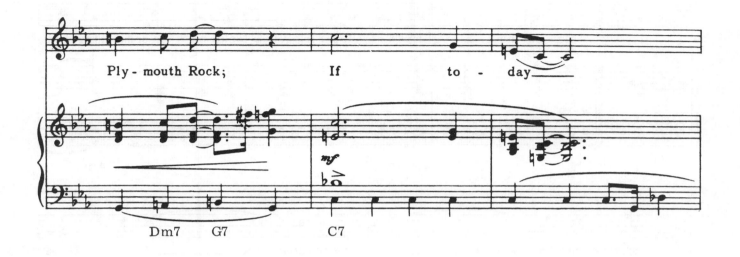

Ply - mouth Rock;   If   to - day____

Dm7   G7   C7

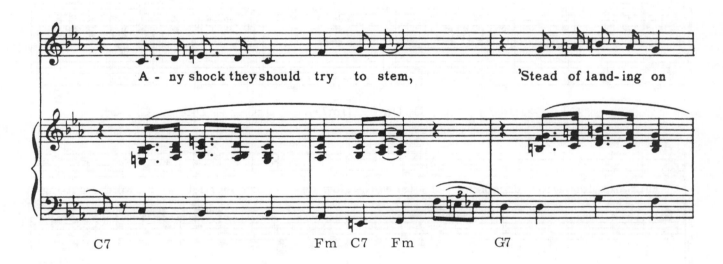

A - ny shock they should try to stem,   'Stead of land-ing on

C7   Fm C7 Fm   G7

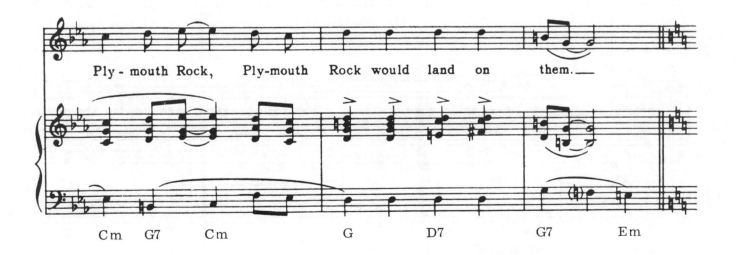

Ply - mouth Rock,   Ply-mouth Rock would land on   them.____

Cm   G7   Cm   G   D7   G7   Em

14

THE BEST YEARS OF MY LIFE

Words and Music by WILL JENNINGS
and STEPHEN ALLEN DAVIS

Verse 2:
When I play my memories again.
I feel all the pleasure and the pain.
Love can hurt, love can heal.
Oh, how we hurt and healed ourselves again.

We took our souls as far as souls can go, ooh yeah.
You've given me the best years of my life.
You've given me the best years of my life.

DON'T GET AROUND MUCH ANY MORE

Words by BOB RUSSELL
Music by DUKE ELLINGTON

FLY ME TO THE MOON

Words and Music by
BART HOWARD

24

FOR ONCE IN MY LIFE

Words by RONALD MILLER
Music by ORLANDO MURDEN

GOLDFINGER

Words by LESLIE BRICUSSE
and ANTHONY NEWLEY
Music by JOHN BARRY

I GOT RHYTHM

Music and Lyrics by
GEORGE GERSHWIN and IRA GERSHWIN

34

REFRAIN (with abandon)

I WON'T LAST A DAY WITHOUT YOU

Words by PAUL WILLIAMS
Music by ROGER NICHOLS

IF MY FRIENDS COULD SEE ME NOW

Words by DOROTHY FIELDS
Music by CY COLEMAN

I'VE GOT YOU UNDER MY SKIN

Words and Music by
COLE PORTER

IN THE MIDDLE OF NOWHERE

Words and Music by
BUDDY KAYE and BEA VERDI

49

THE MAN THAT GOT AWAY

Words by IRA GERSHWIN
Music by HAROLD ARLEN

MY WAY

French Words by GILLES THIBAUT
English Words by PAUL ANKA
Music by CLAUDE FRANCOIS and JACQUES REVAUX

NEW YORK, NEW YORK

Words by FRED EBB
Music by JOHN KANDER

A NIGHTINGALE SANG IN BERKELEY SQUARE

Words by ERIC MASCHWITZ
Music by MANNING SHERWIN

*Pronounced Bar - klee

NO MORE TEARS (ENOUGH IS ENOUGH)

Words and Music by PAUL JABARA
and BRUCE ROBERTS

NO MORE TEARS

It's rain-ing, it's pour-ing, my love life is bor-ing me to tears after all these

years. No sun-shine, no moon-light, no star-dust, no sign___ of ro-

mance, we don't stand a chance. I al-ways dreamed I'd find the

ENOUGH IS ENOUGH

PEOPLE

Words by BOB MERRILL
Music by JULE STYNE

SO FAR AWAY

Words and Music by
CAROLE KING

THERE'S NO BUSINESS LIKE SHOW BUSINESS

Words and Music by
IRVING BERLN

REFRAIN

REFRAIN

WHAT A DIFFERENCE A DAY MADE

Spanish Words and Music by MARIA GREVER
English Words by STANLEY ADAMS

WE DON'T CRY OUT LOUD

Words and Music by
CAROLE BAYER SAGER and PETER ALLEN

cry____ out loud, just keep it in - side, learn__ how to hide your feel - ings.

Fly__ high_____ and proud, and if you should fall, well ba-by you

al - most, you al - most had it all._____

Repeat and fade